CW01083032

the uncorrected billy childish

the un—
corrected

billy
childish

selected poems

chosen with an introduction by **dr albirt umber**
woodcuts by **bill hamper**

the tangerine press • london • 2018

ISBN 978-1-910691-09-0 (paperback)
    978-1-910691-28-1 (hardback)

THIS EDITION FIRST PUBLISHED 2018 BY TANGERINE PRESS
UNIT 18, RIVERSIDE ROAD
GARRATT BUSINESS PARK
LONDON
SW17 0BA
ENGLAND
thetangerinepress.com
PRINTED IN ENGLAND

Tangerine Press books are printed on acid-free paper

Publisher's Note & Acknowledgements

THE UNCORRECTED BILLY CHILDISH was first published in 2009 as a 'Penguin Art Edition' by L-13 Light Industrial Workshop, in tandem with handbound, limited editions by the Tangerine Press. Penguin's lawyers intervened, insisting that all paperbacks were destroyed, resulting in an infamous book burning event in central London. The limited editions are now long out of print and swapping hands for large sums on the collectors' market.

For those readers unfamiliar with its previous incarnations, *The Uncorrected...* differs from the poet's other books in that it has been broken down into themed sections (Fathers & Sons, Love & Sex, Abuse & Forgiveness, Emotional Secretions and so on). Each section also has its own title page, featuring a black and white woodcut illustration by Bill Hamper.

This fully updated and revised selection is taken from various volumes published during the 1980s right up to the present time, alongside previously unpublished new poems. It should also be noted here that Mr Childish is dyslexic and the poems appear as written by himself. Grateful acknowledgement is especially due to the following publishers, where certain of these poems first appeared, sometimes in varying forms: Hangman Books, L-13 Light Industrial Workshop, X-Ray Book Company, Codex Books, Tahoma Books, Sympathetic Press and Blackheath Books. Also the magazines/journals: Bagazine, Dwang, Judas-hole and Wormwood Review.

— MICHAEL CURRAN

other books by billy childish

CONTENTS

'i am billy childish
ex drunk
and compulsive masturbator
late nite vomiter of good liquor
kisser of purple lipped women
riter of poems celebrating the
emptiness of my love
poems hungering for the moment
of my passion
wishing it could allways be so
to never let my cock fall'

Introduction

THE fame of Billy Childish rests not only on his poetry, but also on his paintings, novels and songwriting. He is that most hated of beast in the land: an autodidactic polymath. As all of his art, his poetry is acutely autobiographical, for to Childish his poetry was, in a sense, a logbook of his own emotional universe and experiences. To some extent, that is of course true of all poetry, but there is a difference in the degree to which poets talk about themselves, or talk to themselves. And the early Childish was intensely preoccupied with personal relationships and problems, which he tried to solve in poetic utterance. One of the most decisive influences on his life, for example, was his 'psychological' involvement with his father, a predicament which is referenced to time and again in his novels; and from this dilemma, and the related ones of other intense attachments to women, emerge many of the poems that form the sexual core of this selection.

After expulsion from St Martin's School of Art, in 1981, for writing poetry described by one of his tutors as "the worst type of toilet wall humour I have ever read," he started a relationship with the then fashion student, Traci Emin (later spelled Tracey), and from this vivid emotional experience he wrote a highly personal sequence of poems, which were to become such an important influence on a generation of poets and artists, particularly the yet-to-be 'confessional artist' Tracey Emin, herself.

In much of Childish's poetry, then, the events and crises of his life are summarised with an extraordinary intensity of feeling, but as his powers developed he began to proclaim broader themes. Of these the most insistent was his belief that creativity was man's birthright and that an 'education' that suppressed, or even denied, this birthright was "a lie and corrupt and next to the devil". Beneath the varnish of individuals' accumulated credentials, he believed, was to be found the true picture of human behaviour as God originally intended it, and Childish's vocation (he concluded) was to clean and restore this true expression – as an art expert restores an Old Master. His rhapsodic faith in this philosophy extended beyond its applications to poetry to everyday life, and many of the most passionate poems in this book are revelations into the intense physiological insight Childish commands when he evokes God's nature inherent beneath the "ego shell of man's heart". If poetry is, among other things, an awareness of the visible world, then Childish was abundantly and poetically aware and his forays into Europe, Japan and the United States stimulated him to make poetry out of the everyday sordidness and emotional highs and lows he experienced on these travels. In asserting his philosophy that man's artistic future and happiness lay not in striving for gimmick or originality, but in "grounding oneself in authenticity" and "freedom though limitation", Childish conversely denounced the pretences and evasions of the modern world, and there are many pieces in this selection which reveal his use of poetry for purposes of experimentation, personal revenge, self-deprecation and even self-ridicule.

Whatever view they may take of his merits or excesses, readers of Childish's poems are not likely to condemn them for pussy-footing or shrinking from battle. He does not mince his words anymore than he qualifies his beliefs. He disliked "not naming things by their proper names", and had no time for elegant embellishments of expression, which in some areas are still regarded as the proper coinage of poetry. With the exception of songwriting, Childish never embraced metrical conveniences or devises and expressed himself in 'free' verse. But those with an ear for poetry will observe that, despite the absence of rhyme and patterned rhythms, Childish's poems have a pulse of violent emotional power. His poems were, so to speak, detonated rather than composed and, in his early life at any rate, he was suspicious and impatient with any kind of revision, a process he thought liable to tamper with his stance of "getting out of the way of the picture and letting it paint itself". Childish did not hold with the patient modelling and fashioning of a verse which so many poets declare to be indispensable to their art. He thought that a poem, and indeed all art, was emotionally secreted, and that the poet's job was to refrain from intellectualising it. These rival theories of the nature of creativity will not be argued here, but readers will appraise for themselves the urgent volcanic utterances that were characteristic of this fervent prophet. Those who are familiar with Blake, Walt Whitman and the poetry of D. H. Lawrence will, perhaps, ponder upon resemblances in vision and manner between them and Childish, but, whatever comparisons such speculations may yield, the individuality of Childish will shock and abuse the reader.

— Dr Albirt Umber

There are those who travel down the broad highways of arrogant ambition; others who make their way by base, servile flattery and fawning; and others employ hypocritical deceit; and there are some who take the way of true religion; but I, drawn by my star, travel down the narrow path of knight errantry, which profession leads me to scorn wealth, but not honour.

Don Quijote
— CERVANTES

INSECTS & SMALL CRAWLERS

the little brave ant

a little black ant
has joined me
at table
sucking from tiny
pools of spilt
beer

somhow i feel for
this little
brave one
me wielding pen
and
puffing brimstone

the house is dark
and empty now
just the two of us
joined for this
moment
comrades in drink

your golden hair

that hot still summers
day
when we swam out
till a half mile off shore
then let the slowly
incoming tide carry us
back shoreward

and
we noticed hundreds of
tiny spyders
thousands of them
walking the surffiss
tension
only being capsized
by the ripples we made
whilest treading water

it doesnt seam much now
but back then it did
it seamed like a
miracle

and
the 20 or so i saved
lifted by my wet fingers
to your golden hair
that way
to reach land

the moth

a stark buti will prevail when this earth
is scorched clean of the two-legged ones
a stark buti little moth
a stark buti with no fool of a poet to utter it

and meanwhile i hear dark mutterings
voices of insects
and
the fucking of butterflys

the hoverfly is not a wasp
and you beetle
like a black thumbnail
go back to the woods and rest your
overstuffed head

the names of those ive wished dead

today is the day
to tell of my undisclosed
desire for power
to mention that i have
had sex with a dog
and to utter the names
of those ive wished dead

today is the day
of all the insects
ive tortured
to open my cupped hands
and let go the ants
the wasps and the flies

today is the day
of all the women ive loved badly
to open my delicate heart
and speak of this fear
of women
of spyders
and the night

today is the day
i breathe of my sorrow
hold myself in my arms
with pity
and admit that others live
that they too must be free
to set their own paths
thru hell

ants moths and picaso

little ones
you have come to visit
you love to be near man
and
nest beneath warm concreat
cracked paths are your favorite
you
also walk up the sides of trees
your tiny feet stepping close to
the powdery wings of moths

you carry your dead friends
on your heads
and
once i saw five of you dragging
a dead spyder
under a broken
paving slab to be eaten
by your hungry clan

it is said that on seeing dazzel-painted trucks
driving thru the streets of paris during the great war
picaso pointed and exclaimed
'we (the cubists) are responsble for that'
he didnt mention moths
or zebras at all
thats how we know that he was full of himself

with poems
that
sting
like
wasps

i was in love
with truth
but
not love
with poems that sting like wasps
and
mad men in the sway of false gods

i have been stung
so i too will sting
and
so i stung myself
because truth without love
is the worst type of lying

but
all along
secretly
within this shell
i allways loved love
and now i forgive all
and
see that even a wasp is nothing but
a little winged tiger

a personal history

i hunt death
like a black spyder
like it is a black spyder i mean
a black spyder that i hope
and pray i will not find

what im trying to say is
that i hunt truth
like it is a black spyder
seen
scurrying between a stack
of old bricks
in my fathers back yard

deaths head moth

a nite visiter
came to
the mad house

the artist
looked in wonder
at its colours of amazing distinction
black
gray
cloudy white
tinged with carmine
or vaguely shading off
into olive green

it was a pity
he
had to kill it to paint it
opening his cupped hands
he
flicked its head with his
finger
the moth emited a loud squeek
and fell silent

he arranged it on the nite stand
opening out its powdery wings
he painted feverishly
thru the nite

the beastie was so butil

you moth
are

known as
the severer of the thread of life
the wandering death birds cry
your voice of angish
has been likened
to the
moaning
of
grief stricken children
you honey robber

the painting finished
the artist
sent it along
to his younger brother
thou
the
moths visit
told him
that
nither of them
were
long for this world

20 thousand fleas

she dreamed
it
was all still there
her
clothes
her
paintings
all
sealed
in
that festering basement flat

she
follows
the blud
trail
down
hallway
into the bedroom
yes
the
bed is still there
waiting for sex

on the wall
intricate gravy
stains
dribble to the skirting
from
where
i once slung a fatty roast lamb dinner
up the wall

20 thousand fleas
born of the kitten
she stole
from the tow path in maidstone
in 1984
hop
to bite
at
her brown ankles

BEASTS

some kind of living

bits of life crawling up my feet
jimmy hills on top of adolph
pushing her to the floor
and biting her ears
jimmy squeeks as one of his sisters
comes up from behind and bites
his dick
and they all finish off with
a bit of fuck practice

then they walk over to their mum for
some food
she just sits there
i spose shes drying up
i push her over on her side and the
kittens suckle her tits
little gray eyes and no hope of
living with out that old flea-bag
with her patchy fur and saw nipples

they finish their grub and curl up
on sheilas feet for some kind of
living
some kind of warmth

the dog

the dog
was
dead
and so was her uncle colin
and
she was
stuck in a lift with her arms
crossed
and
the dog
was licking her all over
and
she was
trying to hit the dog with
her crossed arms

i was standing looking down
at her and misscheviously
laughing

this was her dream
not mine

zoo

on a sunny autumn afternoon
we traveled to london
and paid our money
we saw the chimpansees
their women were on heat
the arses pink
and extended
like blocks of meat
the old chimp sniffed at them
and showed them his stiffy
and the schoolgirls giggled

we moved on to the
orang-utang enclosure
theyve got these hands
big sad hands
great hands
and skirts of orange/brown hair
the male checked the womans
cunt under her tresses
he parted the folds and sniffed
then he looked out at us
primevil
human
yes!
undoubtedly human
and
his woman did the same
and
i felt foolish being there
staring dumbly with the crowds
sucking on our ice-creams

a sad donky and a fat man smiling

speaking as a man who doesnt eat cheese
and who paddled into 2nd place in the
kent schools under-18s slalom 1975
(three entrants only)

speaking as a man who doesnt own a television set
doesnt read daily papers
and the radio remains clicked to off

speaking as a man with twelve fillings
four verucas
and one O level (art grade A) walderslade secondry
school for boys 1976

speaking as an artist of dubious merit
and the writer of lewd verses

speaking as a man who caught paul wellers plectrum
thrown into the audience at battersea town hall
jubilee week 1977 (support group the boys)

speaking as a man who carved the reclining admiral
and van gogh without a moustache
apprentice stone mason
her majestys dockyard chatham 1976

speaking as a man who wore second hand shoes
up untill he was 33

speaking as a man who tried to run down johnny rotten
on the pavement outside the roebuck public house kings rd
london 1978 (drunk in charge of a push bike)

speaking as a man with eyes the shape of little fishies
the hands of my father and somebody elses legs
i see that truth only comes staggering up the mountain side
like a sad donky teetering under the weight of a fat man smiling

the first green horse god has made

driving
towards a pink sky
we
pull into the petrol station
i check the oil
and buy 12 pounds worth of petrol
on account that you cant fill the tank becouse
theres a leek half ways up

huddie sits in the car
with my wife julie
and i go in
and
pay

climbing back in
huddie tells me
– i saw a green horse running papa
– a green one really? now theyer unussual
– it was wearing a green coat
explains julie
huddie shakes his head
– no it wasnt it was green
   it must be the first green horse
   god has ever made

where the tiger prowls stripped and unseen

i dont want to here
from my 4 year old son
that there are only
500 thumbless spyder monkeys
left in the wild

or that 3500 albotrosses are killed
each year by the greed of fisherman
by the greed of supermarkets
by the greed of you and me

i want for him to stare in wonder
at the pages of an atlas of the world
and
know that in a far away land named india
there is an inpenitrable jungle
where the tiger still prowls
stripped and unseen

1935 bsa and a small dog

'the bycycle is an invention of genious
the car just an inevitability'

i shave with a cut throat
dress in 80 year old shirts
and
ride thru the night on bycycles

i love art
hate idears
and interests dont interest me

against all the odds
im still here

we zoom thru the traffic
my 2½ year old son siting on the cross bar
– faster pa pa faster! he shouts
– we have to slow down here huddie
i explain
– why?
– because there are people walking
  and we might run them over
– why cant we run them over?
– because we have to respect other people

huddie thinks for a moment
– could we run over a dog? he asks
– no huddie we dont want to hurt
  doggies either
huddie thinks again
– what about a small one? he reasons

the sanity of children

to cross a field and
see a cow pissing
was brillient fun
next was to see a dead mouse
swarming with maggots
or a spyder
eating a fly
but
my favorite was
to see the stallion
over the back fields
straddle
his legs
then slowly telescope
his impossable black cock
down
to the dusty ground

2 jays
a magpie
1 pidgon
1 starling
and a screaming squirrel

across the street from my house
is a long
stand of trees
occupying the dry ditch
of the old fort

foxs live in there
and
the yobs chuck there old sofas
and piss stained matrices
over the spiked railings

this morning
there was a counsel
in the ivy clad trees
2 pinkish jays
were building a nest
shouting at a
a nosey magpie
who in turn
barked at
an enraged screaming squirrel

the pidgon
the starling
and i
stood silently by and just watched

cat facts

for the most part
(once its eaten)
a
cats brain is pretty much
flooded with contentment
thats
obvious

also
cats have a fur coat
and
a tail

something
that not every joe notices
is that rather than
having 4 legs
cats
actually
have
2 back legs
where as
their
front legs
are actually arms

animated stone

im learning love
honestly

you see ive been in the teeth
of deamons
not imagined
but living gargoils
– animated stone springing from the walls

the painters of old nailed their look bang-on
a trident
a spikey tail
clawed feet
a mischievous grimice
even a little pair of hornes
and
some bat wings

and
the drunks
crawling the streets
and
the murderers
and
the simply unhappy
dont know
that they
are dragging a cargo of
animated stone
sprung from walls

some wore crows
tangled in their hair

i walked down the
line
stopping at every man
and
looking into every face
and
every face i recognised

here was my fathers face
here my brothers face
here my grandfathers face
all often repeating
but
every 7th face was plainly myself
and
the hands were my hands
– the prominent wrist bones
somehow bird like
were my wrist bones

it was the hunters
at the end of the line
i envied most
some wore crows
tangled in their hair
and
when i looked into their less worried eyes
it seamed that rather than
growing in vigour
i had somehow been hoodwinked
into
forgetting ease

in the store room
of
the queens own west kent regimental
museum

it was possible
to view a fine
collection of british stuffed birds
including the last buzzed
gunned out the skys of maidstone
sometime in the late 1890s

a gallery of
greenish aquariums
containing
a variety of fresh water fish
that could be found swimming
in the river medway
was arranged over 2 levels

and
in the store room
of
the queens own west kent regimental
museum a small
wiry
ex-cavalry officer
with a clipped white moustache
(the curator)
closed a draw of crimea campaign medals
before turning
clasping the back of a chair
and
thrusting his boney arse into my groin

46

LOVE & SEX

she got it up in the air

she got her arse up in the air
and i got my feet either side of
the bed
and i lowered it in there
my feet astride across the back
of the world
and my hands on hips
then down on her shoulder blades
pushing her face into the pillow
her shaking it from side to side
a little tight ball on elastic strings
and she said – ooh – arrrrh – ooooow –
my stomach hurts when you up there
like that –
like you gonna punch a hole inside
me
and i say –
mmmmmmmm – and it feels like you gonna
split my nob in two
then i try it up her arse a bit
and it gets frantic and its nearly over
a few qwick jerks and its finished
off qwick
i roll off and dose
and theres something wet down there
and shes still playing with my
limp dong
the nites here
the cats are out
and theres funny lumps come up in
my groin

15 qwid

walking thru lester sq
at 10.35pm
with her hard on
my shoulder

i rip up my last 15 qwid
and sprinkle it over
her head
like
confetti

thats the only type
of wedding shes gonna get

soho 1972

i walked with
a childs face
with blind yellow hair
teeth fucked
and chest buckled
with fear

and a businessman
with briefcase and glasses
crosses the road in front of me
turns his mangled face and says
– this is a sexy place
   isnt it?

the page of love

mend and sow
draw with these words
knit a unity

let the ink flow
the letters dance
and the s's smile

here is peace for
broken princesses
for the gun-wed
and de-harted

here is bandage
for bludded thoughts
and breast to calm
all maladie

where sister meets
brother
where brother holds
sister
and each knows
the rite to hold
themselves in love

waterloo station

– ive been ill
  i was ill all last year
  i split up with chris
  i had an abortion
  it was twins and
  they cut them up inside
  of me
  and two days later
  a little arm came out
  whilst i was sitting
  in the taxi
  but i wont tell you
  about it cos youll
  only go and blab about it
  in one of your stupid poems

she glared at me
hungry and broke
and i understood
that what i loved about
this woman
was the depth of her spite
and anger
she hated the world
she hated men
and she hated me

i handed her a twenty
and watched her stupid
face light up

shell remember all of my
indiscreditions
but never the gift
of this poem

53

chatham town welcomes desperate men

welcome the nite watchman
the floor polisher
the dole-queue boy
and
the policeman in the rain

welcome the salesman who never sells
the dentist who hates teeth
the docker without a dock
and
the robber of car hub-caps

welcome lovers who cannot love
lickers of bright green ice lollies
motherless children
and
the smashers of car wing mirrors

welcome achne
toothache
kabab shop owners
used-car salesmen
and
the buyers of second hand fridges

welcome the sailor from a far away land
and try not to punch him on the nose
welcome pimps prostitutes
and
a smiling dose of the clap

welcome larger drinkers
with tattoed fists

and the bare nuckle fighters of
kent
irland
romany
and
beyond

welcome the uneducated and the lost
welcome teachers too sceared to teach
welcome office werkers
wild 3 legged dogs
and
the smiling of hell

welcome cigaret smokers
hash smokers
pen pushers
stollen car drivers
garage attendents
shelf stackers
shelf haters
heroin users
and
girls in white calf length boots

welcome the men of middle management
their bored house wifes
and
alcoholic children in private schools

welcome till girls with love-bites

welcome gray skys and icy winds
welcome magpies and crows
welcome con-men and the conned
and

children with flick-knives

welcome men in envy
town planners
councilers of little faith
and
old ladies in faded blue coats

welcome estate agents bearing
false gifts
and dressed in fake pin-stripe suits

welcome the owners of lawns
car show rooms
impossable morgages
and
bank managers who can no longer manage

welcome the indebted and the owners of naught

welcome one eyed cats
and panthers in the nite
welcome circus tricksters
casuel labourers
and crawling curb crawlers

welcome liers
cheats
and
fornicators
welcome poets smiling thru their teeth
welcome dead novelists and
sunken battle-ships
welcome men in blazers from nepal

from the tax office of limehouse reach

to the dole queue of the brook
chatham town welcomes desperate men
it loves you all
and
honeres you all

at midnite i will say i love you

in this house tonite
insects dance
the walls holding up the nite
and spyders
viberate in their webs
laughing

lying beneath
the old pump organ
is the mumified corps
of a poisoned mouse
killed
by an ex-girlfriend

all i have left to say
is that i am sorry
or rather
that i am angry that
you think that
i should say
that i am sorry
but
i am sorry

it is true
that the furniture
is busted
and the carpets are filthy
but i dont want to
worry about furniture
or muddy feet or hoovering
or head aches or moskito bites
or the kings

and queens
of
art
and
fashion

do you know something
next doors cat
used to come
and sit on my shoulders
whilest i was riting
she was black and friendly
called tibbs
but i renamed her
mister tibbs
then she got fleas
and the old girlfriend
banished her
from the house
next
the phone shivers
into life
and
afraid of aloness
i ansewer

it is midnite
and
i will say that
i love you
even if
i have to lie

fort pitt whores

coming off the roundabout
i see a hitch-hiker
i pull over
shes about 15 or 16
dressed like a whore
wants a lift to new rd

– i aint on drugs
   i aint got a bloke
   i look after myself
   its good money
   20 qwid a hand job
   25 a blow job
   35 with tits
   and 50 for full sex
   i aint been raped yet
   but one nite
   this fella drives me out to cooling
   on the marshes
   he thretens me
   but i jumped out the car and
   just legged it

– how do you know whos alright to go with
   and who isnt?
i ask

she looks at me from her childs face
– i dont
she says
– i just get in

keeping an eye out for police cars

i pull over
at the bottom
of fort pitt hill
– look after yourself
i say
– me and my wife come this way
  if we see you we will say hello
  a lot of people arnt so nice to the girls

– yeah
she says
and
gives a little wave as i crawl up the hill
in my dying 1968 volvo

pure as spring water

we were lying in bed
the sheets hot and wet with
our bodys
the sunlite coming in
some birds singing

– i am as pure as the
   purist spring water
and as i speak i can feel
its true
my mind a fine edge
undirtyed as a childs

– you aint pure your full
   of diseases

and she goes to hit me
i hold her arms back and
roll my waight onto her
she struggles and i laugh
in her face
she spits at me

– you make me sick
   i told you i didnt want
   you to bring me anything
   back from germany
   but you brought me
   girlfriends and gonnareah

i look down into her twisted
mouth but nothing can spoil
my mood

i carnt feel angry i can
only laugh pure peals of
laughter
pure as the purist spring
water

he is mine

wriggling in idiocy
i birthed an idiot child: me
oh how
i loved that little retard
oh how
i kissed him
1st
i taught him how to walk
then
nurturing him on whisky
and
sugared ciggerets
suddenly he somehow
vomited into my open mouth
whoops!
disgusting!
but hay
thats how i taste him
thats how i
know that he is mine
and
oh how i love that little retard
oh how i kiss him

he wanted to be a famouse poet
she wanted his spunk

he trained her to drink it daily
told her it would help her stupid mind
he was rong
she wanted to suck him dry
but nothing could refresh that dryed out walnut
so he jumped out of bed and walkt the mile home
dragging her along behind him
thru the midnite park
her clinging to his legs in her nighty

he thort
this is what living is all about
again
he was rong

meditation

city the arse
hillside the tits
my spunk falls
like
warm snow

i love my wifes cunt

– i love her cunt!

what drives the creation
but sex and becoming?
so i proclaim it

– i love her cunt!

why else would god tie me to it?
no one need know it
but
still i proclaim it

– i love her cunt!

i revel in its folds and intricasys
i revel in its aroma and flavour
in its lushness and sweetness

– i love her cunt!

i am loud
overbearing
and talk
too freely and liberally
and
rite this poem
in gods hand

– i love her cunt!

i am in love with her cunt
with its perfection

its completeness and adequacy
so
i kneel to it as an alter
licking
and
admiring

why else would god tie me to it?

scout

my 3 year old daughter pronks
across the room
singing
add-libbing in joy
indescribable love
engulfs me

ABUSE & FORGIVENESS

a mad noise like birds

– ive got to tell you
she said
– i didnt abort that baby
  i wouldnt abort that baby
  i admit i drank a lot
  and wore my belt tight
  but i didnt abort that baby

– i lost it 2 days after you
  picked me up by the stomach
  and threw me across the floor
  im not saying its your fault
  i didnt tell you i was pregnent
  becouse i was scared youd
  call me irresponsible
  but i didnt abort that baby
  i wouldnt
  im not saying its your fault
  but i lost it 2 days after
  you threw me across the floor
  by my stomach

her voise kept going faster
faster and faster
a mad noise like birds

– be quiet… i gasped
  be quiet be quiet

– i dont understand how or
  what your riteing she said
– i dont understand why

thick as thieves

the beer bottles line up
on the table
like people
like pieces of a chess set
like a row of preachers
like soldiers on parade
like a conspirisy
thick as thieves
and
on
the
sofa
drunk
with the table at eye level
lying like this
they are moving
talking
amongst themselves
coming towards me
acusing me
and
i let them come
for they are none other
than my little brothers

being 10 years old

and shouting as hard
as you can
hopeing to lose
your voise
wanting to be a
tyranosorous-rex
or a squirrel
and 2 weeks holidays
at seasalter
and allways hanging
round the pub doorway
till gone 11
and the grown-ups feeding
us on pop and crisps
and odd coppers for
the one-armed bandits
and allways being shoved
by that barstard brother
of mine
till it was chucking-out time
and wed all head back
to the shack
and us kids with so much
brass in our pockets
we could hardly hold
our shorts up

and in the carpark nearly
losing my thumb in the
slam of uncle normens
car door
and him patting my arse
and grinning down at me thru

his evil little specks
and me allready shitting
myself
knowing that when we
got back
id have to wank his
cock

remember the forgotten

10 pink toes
10 pink little toes
and one crushed and all askew

where be her hands now
where her hart and hair
the braided and the combed
where be her teeth and tongue
speaking with others now
uttering foreign names

and on the mantle piece
2 hair bands lay discarded just as
she left them
2 golden hallowed child-like things
a hair still twisted remembering the yellow
shock of her head

remember the forgotten sorrowed man
hold trinkets in your palm
pick thru these desperate remains
bow your head and kiss the wounds

kiss the damp hairs
kiss her thighs
kiss her feet
10 pink toes
10 pink little toes
and one crushed and all askew

thumb print

i wore an american sailors cap
and cupped my hands to my
snaggled teeth as i grinned in
this photo he clicked

a 9 year old kid handled
by this 40 year old man
his unkind grasp
and fake friendliness still
walk in my sleep
his thumbprint indellible
upon my childs spine

and i would like to ask
but one question of you father
of you mother

– where were you my brave
   protectors?
and i see you kissing in other
peoples arms
in cheap bars
oblivious
loving only your own pain

i give myself to them all

i walk towards this nite
towards the drunkards
and the lost
towards the sluts
and the broken of
hart
in hard bitten bars
between dog-ends and bad scotch
sucking on bitter cigars
and dreams of bitter
whores
and i give myself to you all
to these piss soaked walls
and kicked in doors

you of purple breath
you of painted flesh
you of dusky flesh
you of hated tits and arses
come be in my poems
for ive come to write you all
you shit eaters
and you beaten
you ridiculed and despised
yes you espesherly
come bring your voices
and we will walk arm in arm
thru this whore of a town
towards the stinking river
and the dawn
and
our dreams shall prove no less poetic
our love no less true

and
our kisses be as sweet
as dog rose

for here all are welcome

poisonus women

flint eyed
unable to love yourselfs
unable to love the world
unable to love me
how i loved you all
for i felt safe
how i gathered you to my bosom
like moths

abused by your fathers
and thumbling men
mirroring my
own
trampled hart
i
rote you my softest
most violent poems
and conquered you all
with my skill at sex
and the pen
and i painted you too
old
and ugly
for the futcher to see

you said you loved me
and only me
and i was happy
to believe that
exciting
prepostrious lie

but

i dont blame you for failing me
for failing yourselfs and the world
for failing love
for
i love you all still
my poisonus women
but i wont sip from your mouths
and cunts no more

ode to the endless motorways

scattered with the rainbowed shells
of bugs and beetles
built with the juce of ancient forests
and bones of the fallen
bringing worlds to us
and stealing worlds from us
a happy road
a black scar of a road

like a tarmac river
littered with dead foxs
guarded by crow and hawk
cutting thru chalk
cutting through forest
and dreams
marrying minds and diminishing minds
celibrating banality
and mediocraty
leading to the sky ways
and stars ways
to werk
home
and lost ones
and found ones
escapes
joinings and funerals

racing from one
unsavoured moment to the next
from unhappiness
into the arms of unhappiness
the world reduced to
a painted backdrop

to a film
staring only us
to our drama
our poem
our missery
laughing
joyusly
blotting out death
then slowing
at junction 6
to servay anothers carnege

sat motionless in log jams
planning conquests
and hating our enimys
and gods rhitchiousness
yes
and
roads to god
to devils and commerce
roads to hope and glory
caesars highway
and hitlers autobarns
for roads have allways been built
to wage war
to take young men
and promise never to give them back

the forgiveness of peadophiles

i will try to forgive you
as i will try to forgive myself
and
i send a kiss to your
daughter susane
she who you never fucked
though you fucked me
but it is she who is
in the mad house
and
i am here in this nite
writing this
difficult poem

did you know
norman
that thou you never touched her
your 11 year old daughter
used to suck the cock of her
friends father
yes
he fucked both of them
when your daughter came to visit
he used to send his daughter up to bed
and
concentrated on susane

his daughters name was joe anne
and
i was 9
and
i loved her
i repeat – i was aged 9

and
needed a fathers protecting hand
not your hairy fist up my shorts

bed wetter

12 years old i still pissed the bed
i pissed in anger at my mother
i pissed in fear
i pissed in love lacking
i pissed in desperation
i pissed in grief
i pissed in aloneness
i pissed in need of specialness
i pissed in sexual anticipation

still a child
not held
but touched by
a mans whoery hand
wounded in the hart – a gap – a hole clean thru
i pissed in wondering
where the angels were
vampires id seen

the day is begging for your kiss

i will be waiting outside the old school gates
where you came that day to abduct me
i will have no gun concealed in my pocket
just my harmless white fist

if you here the birds singing
think of me
of how you wanted to take
me to the woods
and kill me
if you see matted hair in the plug hole
think of me
if you see a car go past
think of me
or a plain in the sky
or trees
or grass
or 2 dogs fighting
or fucking
or a childs face at a window
that will be good
or
as you look at the backs of your old hands
think of me
becouse
i am still here
and though in your mind
i am still only a child
i am not a sex object
but a man

the mirror of the poem

the mirror
in
the darkened room
curtens drawn
i
finger my mothers lipstick
here on the dressing table
i
smell the soft blud redness
paint my lips
and
undress

i
put on her bra
stockings
and
suspenders
a green wool suit
fits
a headscarf for my blond shoulder length
hair
and
in her handbag
a powder pack
i apply mascara
lastly
a pair of heels
and im 12 years old
and
ready to walk the streets

i still write for that mirror

the ornate mirror
the opaque mirror
the aged
clouded mirror in the darkened room

FATHERS & SONS

my father

my father was absent
my father used to spend 300 qwid
on fucking the fatist uglyist
whores
my father was a drunked
my father beat my mother
my father was afraid of his father
my father was a failure
my father was a criminel
my father was unhappy
my father was a mad man

and when i punched him
down stairs
the bruise came up under his
left eye
and crawled down his cheek
like a purple slug

primary school tough

there was frost on the tarmac
that december morning
and my cap was pillarbox red
badged with acorns and sat
upon my blond head
and
i walk in long grey socks
and hand-me-down shorts
of my brother
my fathers tie knotted at
my throat

it was december the first 1964
and little andrew walked proudly
by my side
and to every passing person
would announce
– this is my friend steven
  he is five years old
  today

huddie 8.12.99

huddie
i may be the stangest father
but i welcome you
your grandmothers welcome you
your grandfathers welcome you
your brothers
and your sisters welcome you
we all welcome you
you belong here

huddie
after 14 years me and keerah decided to part
the last nite we slept togther
was the nite you were conceveed
we didnt chose you
you chose us
and we rejoiced

but for 4 months
we didnt even know you were in there
when keerah finnaly found out
she was pregnent
i got down on my knees
and kissed her belly
– hello i said
– i know a lot of stange
　things have been going on out here
　but theyer nothing to do with you
　you are still wanted
　you are welcome
and
5 months later
on a cold morning in december

i arrived at the hospital
wearing my hat and clutching carrier bags
and
a flask of hot tea
i entered the room
keerah was sat astride a chair in labour
i put down my bags
kissed her
then walked to the window
4 stories up
i looked out over this bleak river
a rain-swept view from rochester to hoo
and
below us tucked under the hillside
my ugly home town

i suddenly recognise why i have remained
stuck in this landscape when the rest of my family
have long since qwit it
my brother has qwit it
my father has qwit it
and my mother too
im the only one to remain
except my grandperents
who lay buried in these chalk hills

for how many thousands of years
have i looked out over this muddy estery?
since before the romans came?
– certanly
i see myself as a warrior chieften
born here again and again
deposed by romans
deposed by my own clan
fighting to keep my footing
against slimy betrails

so i am caught by this land
by the siloet of these familiar hills
my family may run
but im the one who has been left here to desolve the past
and put these ancient ghosts to rest
and you
sweet huddie
who have been my son many times before
are ment to be here with me

me and keerah didnt bring you into being
you willed yourself into being
this warrior chief has just been waighting for your return

your mother is a brave woman
huddie
she made a butifull plan for you to be born at home
in the most simple way
to incence burning
and
holy music playing
but instead you came into this world arse first
and the doctors wanted to drug her and cut you from
her belly
but your keerah insisted on giving birth and letting you
decide when your entrance should be
she refused all drugs
wishing to keep your blud pure

as her time drew near
i helped her up onto the table
the doctor came and shone a lite
which i fancied was too bright
then i saw your bum sat
deep in keerahs virgina
5 little wite toes

shortly
2 surgons came to view
this strange flemish woman who refused
all pain releaf
and lying there on her back
she lifted her head
and
ordered them to leave the room
then suddenly a whole foot appeared
and
the doctor grasped your legs
and
pulled till i thought he would snap you
in two
quickly your back showed purple
it seamed you were already born
but then your head stuck fast

i mopped keerahs brow
and
the doctor gave her a nasty snip
took up his forceps
and pulled you out like a skinned rabbit
he
plopped you
there on to keerahs wite belly

– i have a baby gasped keerah
and
i staired at you in wonder

is it really possable that we all come into this world
in this same way?
murderers
bus conductors

tax collectors
and
saints?
how can one being be alive in another?

– my baby!
   i have a baby! keerah sobbed again
and we loved you huddie
with such intencity
the same as we loved you when we first learned
that you were hiding
in keerahs womb
i held you in my arms
as they stiched keerah painfully together again
and spoke with you
letting you know that everything was alright
telling you all those things
that i had once longed to here

you are so butifull huddie
you came into this world
to teach me love
and
i welcome you

you will not be abused
as i was abused
i will not allow it
you will not be told you are ugly
as i was told i was ugly
or that you are backwards or stupid
if you are slow to riting or mathmatics
then damn riting and mathmatics
you will not be told you cryed too much
or that you were too clingy or needy
as i was told i cryed too much

and was too clingy and needy
love cannot spoil a child
if you wish to sing then you shall sing
if you wish to dance then you shall dance
and you will not be told you have a god-awful voice
or that you are tone deaf
or that you have 2 left feet
your desire to be will be your reason to be

yes huddie
you are honered and adored as a child born
i may be the strangest father
but i welcome you
your grandmothers welcome you
your grandfathers welcome you
your sisters welcome you
and your brothers welcome you
you belong here
and
i will allways be here for you
the man who thought he would never be a father is a father

the man who thought
he would never
be a father
is
a father

the man who thought
he would never hold a child in his arms
holds a child in his arms
holds him to his aching hart

and when i hold you
and perseve you in your open wonder
of the world

it is allmost too painful for me
i too remember being as open and blessed as you
and every movement of your breath
i too remember making that movement
and the movements are one

and every pain of parting
with your mother
i too remember the pain of that parting
with my mother
when i see the golden light that surrounds you
i too remember that golden light
and i understand why my
nanna lewis called me
'her angel'

and when i hold you in these
supple arms
i realise that i too hold myself
every gentle part of your buti
is my buti
your eyes that carry no darkness
are my eyes
your lips that want to know every sensation
are my lips
and as i cradle you to my chest
my heart shudders
and
i think of life and death
and
wonder at how these two mysterys
are linked hand in hand
and think of what special promis
i want to give you

that promis is of my undying love

which my father could never give to me
but which flows from me to you
so painfully and so easyly
these are my feelings
becouse i am your father
the man who never thought
he would be
a
father

my son shows me who i once was

i show my son a picture
of myself
aged 3
– whos this huddie
i ask
– huddie
he says
and
i laugh
lift him to my arms
put my lips to his golden hair
and breathe him
and kiss the back of his kneck
he kicks and struggles
i put him down
and he runs up the corridor
and back down again calling
– papa papa
and jumps back into my arms

i feel the life darting within him
and a feeling of such joy and sadness
struggles up from my chest
that it threatens to strangle me

and
then
to imagine a broad-sword in my hand
and suddenly – with one blow –
i take off the head of norman
the 42 year old man
who abused me

and
i marvel that such love and anger
is within me
then celibrate
for i know that i after all am human
and
am now a man

john in west whittering

mornings my father walks
the beaches of west whittering
picking rubbish
for the local council
he likes the big skys

he has another little job in the afternoons
doing telly sales for a greatings cards firm
in the evening he takes his medication
dreams of turner
and paints the whitterings

acording to him he doesnt drink any more
i listen to his slured voice on the phone
his new wife has left him
and weekends my 8 year old brother
goes to stay with him in his council flat

i am the only member of the old family left
who will even speak with him
– i am a recluse he explains to me
the truth is that
my father is the most ungiving person
i have ever met
yet he gave me life

mallory and shackelton

– papa i think i liked the cats best
   when they were still kittens

– whys that huddie?

– because they were more playful

– yes kittens are more playful

– i think i like malory best
   because he was the most playful
   of the kittens when we chose him

huddie looks at me thortfully

– did i choose him papa?

– yes i think you helped choose him

– i think im more like mallory as well
   because mallory doesnt like trying new things
   does he
   and he likes going off exploring
   and i dont like trying new things and i like
   exploring
   and mallory comes when you call him
   whereas shackleton doesnt
   and id come if you called me papa
   thats why im more like mallory

only my father

it all happened outside
newcoms – shirt makers to the king
of
course this
was before they
knocked the arse out of the town
putting in a flyover
that
no one wanted

i
saw him
crossing the street
towards me
yes it was deffinetly him
thou
who would have thort
that he could still exist
in the outside world

and
such tiny feet
for a man of his hight
he was all dressed up
like hed just escaped from
an
edwardian wax werks

he then tried to avoid
aknowleging me
as we were in public
but
i still made him say hello

– who the fuck was that?
asked my mate
staring after him

– that? no one
  only my father

IN NATURE

fat nature

so whats this nature i heard people
talking about
the children crying about
some sexual nature
some human nature
squirrels – murders – perverts nature
a big fat nature for us all

i smoked some naturel cigerets
i drank some naturel wisky
i read some naturel porn

i saw some fucking freek with a beard
and a weetabix jumper waveing a board
above his head
i saw some fucking freek telling the
end of the world

i got into some naturel tv
eat a naturel sossage made from pigs
cock and brains
killed by a naturel man earning his
money
i had a naturel egg layed by a naturel
chicken stuck in a six inch box

and im gonna die naturely
in front of some car
a failed kiddny
brain hemerage
a 60 megaton bomb
every damn bit of it nature

poem

it wasnt a rose
in winter
it was a dirty piece
of tissue cought
in a hawthawn bush
but somehow it was
better than a rose

a matter of life and death

i walked out into the garden
i saw a large spyder lying on
its back
twitching one leg
it was in the throws of its
own death

and the dog was on its lead
jerking itself off

i kicked the dog
and walked back into
the house

a big soft dog of a poet

im no hard man
im a big soft dog of a poet
desperate for people to like me
a damaged broken dog of a poet
a half-man pierced by arrows

more sensitive than a school girl
more prone to upsets
alive with vengeances
more dangerous than a wounded wolf
telling tales on self and others then whining for mercy

an angry chimp of a poet
rageing thru the jungle
hanging upside down
thirsty for monkey brains

a lying thieving rat of a poet
who hates poetry
who will not be a poet for you
for your mother your lover or anyone

a lovable kitten of a poet
tigerish and selfish
whose verses are as harmless as milk

an ant of a poet
acid-mouthed and creeping
the type of charlatan who will deny
hes wearing a hat whilst wearing a hat

coelacanth

old 4 legs comes up river
swims in under the 2 columned bridge
and finds himself a mermaid sat
there on the muddy bank

wagging his oily tail
old 4 legs drags himself up the forshore
and nudges her in her mermaids hip

the memaid looks down
upon old 4 legs
smiles and lifts him to her lap
where she good naturedly
breast feeds him

how else do you think man
came to walk with dogs
smoke cigerets
and play chess
less he was born of a fish

this day gleaming like a gun

the sun 4 hours high
jewled in ragged blue

see the river curl like a worm
in the palm of your hand
see gasomiter and muddy wurl
see strood and frindsbury beyond

see its nearness
its distance
its space
see it joined and far flung

see chatham stranded
broken at the throat
see rochester below
still snaked in mist
see castle keep and cathedral spire

see its nearness
see its distence
see its space
see it joined and far flung

see the exhorst of lorrys rise
like the fountainous breath of ponys
see that which you deserve
see this day gleaming like a gun

we saw a cloud

in the shape of a horse
upon its back
was a helmeted soldier
as we looked it grew in detail
until we could see
the horses bared teeth
then the sun
picked out the scull head
of the ryder
and
he grinned down upon us
and the horse
and soldier
were no longer cloud
and vapour
but rotting flesh
and bare bone
and skelington
of a mounted german soldier
he loomed enormous
and
i knew that he was the spirit
of all the german
dead of the great war
and
i called the others who
were with me
to bow their heads
for this spirit wasnt smiling
from his scull mouth
but screaming
and
he needed prayers
not gaupers

huddie and the moon

huddie waves to the postman
to the taxi driver
to any plane that flys over
or to birds
to passing cars
and tonite
outside the kitchen window
he waves to the full moon
huddie wants the moon to come closer
he beckons
he holds out his potato
towards the moon
he wants to give the moon a potato
huddie is one year old
so he tells everything by sign
he wants the key to the back door
he wants to go out into the garden to be near the
moon
then he wants kcerah to unfold his pram
so that they can drive to the moon
keerah explains to huddie
that the moon is a very
long way away

the snow

for robert walsa

an old man looks out the
window at the snow
he drinks his milk
and
sets off
he walks out into the
snow
ploughing thru the drifts
like a battle cruser
thru ice cream

the snow is falling
the old man wears gloves
and
a hat
and
on the end of each
magnificent calf
spouts a nailed boot

the old man has an
apointment
with death
the snow hurtles past his
nose
the old man looks
puzzeled
he is about to fall down
and
let his hat roll clean
away

nite ash

whilst
stood naked
taking a nite piss
i would often look from my bog window
into your strange arms
glistening in the lite of the street lamp

guarding the bishops graveyard
something
in your towering majesty
reminded me
of death

dressed in your nice greenery
shadows pooled in your embrace
like you were rooted in the bitter water
of some southern swamp
yes
thats how it was –
as if i was looking into
a dark reflection

till 3 men came
in yellow hats
and
cheep looking boots
and
hacked you down

tryfen snowdonia

mid january
dressed
in
wool trousers
70 year old nailed boots
moth eaten puttys
and
a waterlogged wind sheeter
i
battle up a blind gully in snowdonia
with
the boards for our painting trip
strapped to my back
meanwhile
a friendly blizzard flings snow in under the brim of my
panza ski cap
it is mid january
and
i
am 55 years old
suffering from prostatitis
and
my fingers have stopped
operating

at segantinies hut

many people
laboured here
cutting a path
that
zig-zags up
between jagged rocks

this
must be the route
segantinie lugged his canvass
to the top

you
mite think this
would be the province
of mountain goats
but
here we pass black alpine cows
chewing the cud on the
45 degree slope
every
year 2 or 3
black shape it into the valley bellow
cow bells clanging

we breast the top
here is segantinies hut
where he died of acute peritonitus
i was expecting
a ruin
or
perhaps a museum
not a café surving
bacon and eggs

we sit in
bright cold sunshine
it is good to be here
to eat
and
not yet be a dead artist

the occasional cow bell
sounds from the mountain side bellow
and
the
distant rumble is
not a jet
but
a far flung glacia
talking

an oak leaf garland

anyone would think
there
was a war to be
faught
and
won
i wriggle my damaged toe
in my
nailed boot
a sprig of acorns in my hat
above me
a mighty oak
behind
and
to the front
yellow birch line
their silver bows glistening in drizzel
but
there is no war
just
my feet rustling
last years leafs
as i
piss on dead oak

the quiet steam riseing like stags breath

WITH & WITHOUT GOD

old lady down town

as i turned the corner i saw an
old lady lying in the gutter
a small crowd had gavered to watch
you could see pretend death on the
tv every half hour but this was
the real thing
her face looked as if some deamon
had just sucked up her only child

wite face and purple lips
with some bloke snogging her
blowing life in or out
and all her clean cloaths all dirty
with the street muck

her stockings got those same little
splashes on them as her little school
girl socks must of had all them
years ago

dead in hamburg killed in koln

1
i was dead in hamburg
killed in koln
that little girl who looked not
a day over 14 but was 21 and had a
name like a flying boat
her eyes looked at my mouth
and when i kissed her she had to
stand on my knees

a little girl pulling at my trouser
leg – asking for her tea
i walked into the washing line in
my room
a wet shirt slapped across my back
and i fell in the waist bin

2
a woman cut in half
aranged in the bath with the legs
one way round n the body the other
way
submerged in water
the legs hanging over the edge with
maybe one stileto heel
the other foot could be missing

3
ive been seeing little mites again
i spose they live off my toenail
clippings
the bits of blood i leave lying round

when i get undressed i shake all that
skin off my body and they come
running and eat it up

letter from a potential psycopath

3 years old
i stood on the kitten
and tried to break her back
i held the gold fish in the
palm of my hand till it
wriggled free and fell back
in the bowl
i just couldnt believe it was
alive

as a child
i banged my head on the bathroom wall
and 4 foot up
are 2 smashed tiles

i made the family dog lick
my cock
i held it in the palm of my
hand then i tossed onto thc floor
i strangled the dog till he
stopped breathing
then let him go and he went
and lapped it up with a rasping
noise in his throat

at 16
i clubbed my hand a ½ dozen times
with a 4lb club hammer to get
a week off werk

today
i stood behind my father
clenching an iron poker

grinding and breaking my
back teeth
this is normal
i am a healthy 22 year old

like a god i love all things

her name was toshie
– and what does toshie
   mean?
i asked her
– given quickly and
   sensitivly
she tells me

and i laughed and over
the year we became lovers
(only i am no lover)

her 25 years old and never
given to another man
– but how do you feel?
she asks me

– you never tell me how
   you feel… do you love
   me?

and just that word love
makes sadness step from
my mouth and i think

of course i love you
like a god i love all
things

the bitter cup *(song)*

and i remember the breath of my father
his kisses were bearded and damp
the romance of the bottle dragging him down
to awaken disheveled in the tank

and theres no sea deeper than the piss of the bottle
and none speaks the truth like the drunk
wisky runs thru me like a sorrowful river
im down on my knees and im sunk

and i remember my mother hitting the gin
she fell and we thought she was dead
naked and doll-like
his skull face was shouting
we ran to our room painted red

hot for women we curse and abuse them
they say we aint got no respect
full of bravado godless and fearful
we pray no one will detect

and theres no taste sweeter than the rush of hot vomit
seived thru decaying back teeth
id wisper i love you
and qwit all his hating
but in truth i aint got the belief

smashed and disheveled
of course they did wreck us
poisoned by our own bitter cup
stumbling and hoping inside i was lonely
im sick and im down and
im drunk

i am the strange hero of hunger

my girlfreind lives
on the other side of the world
and
has
started
reading
crime and punishment
by fydor dostoyevski

– do you recognise the main chariter?
i ask her excitedly
– doesnt he remind you of me?

– ive only just begun
she ansewers
– whats his name?

– rodya
  but all the characters
  have about 3 diffrent names
  i allways get confused
  and
  cant tell who is who
  becouse im dislexic and dont make sounds for the names
  but rodya is for short
  and
  his sister is called dunya
  isnt dunya a butifull name?
  if little huddie had been born a girl
  we would of named her
  dunya

when i talk of the buti

of girls names
or the strange bravery
of artists
or see
the lite change
over sea
and sky
every second impossable showers of
gold
turning to terrible hues of purple
and
black
and
my
hart rate quickens
becouse
i am amongst
my
own
people

i am
the hero of all my favorite novels
i live in them
and they
live in me
i am arturo bandini
on angels flight
swearing at a butifull dark haired girl
in tattered shoes
i am rodya
guilty of a terrible and senceless murder
on the streets of st petersburg
i am the strange hero of hunger
starving to spite myself in chrsitiana
i am johan nagel

tormentor of the midget
and suiside
i am ishmail
knocker off of tall hats
i am every novelist
and
every charicter ever dreamed
i am everyone of my favorite artists
and
i feel myself not one jot less
but equell to all of them
turner
munch
holbine
and
hokusi

naturally i have no heros
i am my heros
i am my brothers
and sisters
i feel myself joined by the soul
with all buti
my hart sings with every brave endevor
with the strange wings of impossable butterflys
with every rock that breaths life into the world

i stand shoulder to shoulder with
all denoucers of meaness
i honour spirit and faith
and i uphold the glorious amateur
i am in love with desperate men
with desperate hands
walking in 2nd hand shoes
serching for god
and

hearing god
and hating god
i am a desperate man buckled with fear
i am a desperate man who demands to be listend to
who demands to connect
i am a desperate man who denounces
the dullness of money
and status
i am a desperate man will not bow down to acolayed or success

i am a desperate man who loves the simplisity of painting
and hates gallarys and white walls and the dealers in art
who loves unreasonableness
and hot headedness
who loves contradiction
hates publishing houses
and
also i am vincent van gogh
hiroshige
and every living breathing artist
who dares to draw god
on this planet

i am an angry man

angry enough to have killed my father
angry enough to destroy goldfish in the palm of my hand
angry enough to have sex with a dog
angry enough to burn holes in the backs of my hands like
melting plastic
angry enough to threaten myself with death
angry enough to drive a car without oil
angry enough to kill wasps slowly
angry enough to never read another newspaper
angry enough to clean toilets in the house of the mad
angry enough to drink poison
angry enough to denounce god as a liar
angry enough to clean my teeth till my gums bleed
angry enough to make 6 hundred drawings
in the tea huts of hell
angry enough to mock policemen in the nite
angry enough to smash plates and stab myself in the foot
angry enough to set fire to my desk
angry enough to walk with stones in my shoes
angry enough to hate all celebrity
angry enough to stare into the sun
angry enough to punch myself in the nose
angry enough to blow my fingers off with a firework
angry enough to refuse to become famous
angry enough to threaten the dead
angry enough to cook a meal for my enemies
angry enough to polish my fathers rolls royce with paint
stripper
angry enough to welcome my girlfriends lovers
angry enough to fall in love with women who
despise me
angry enough to smash my hand with a 4lb club hammer
angry enough to skin a rabbit

angry enough to punch my typewriter
angry enough to boil a kettle dry
angry enough to swallow my tongue
angry enough to inspire the contempt of the righteous
angry enough to over wind a pocket watch
angry enough to name the names of those ive wished dead
angry enough to tell all of the secrets of my lovers
angry enough to deny myself everything
angry enough to have twelve bad teeth
angry enough to say nothing

the jewesses hand in formaldehyde

he was an art school lecturer from strasbourg
and wore excessively tight jeans
with his french cock and balls
pinned out beneath the cloth

had a tall dark-haired sexual girlfriend
(one of his students)
who looked at my paintings
and told me that i didnt know how
to draw a real womans breasts
– you havent seen the breasts
i answered

i slept on their sofa
in the centre of the room was an ancient dentists chair
of cracked leather
under which he masturbated a pet dog
and there was a horse whip propped there
for whacking his girlfriends buttocks

in the morning i got up and made tea
and sitting on the fridge was a speciman jar
containing a childs severed hand
its blackened finger nails and little feathers of grey skin
wafting like anemones in the formaldehyde

– its from a local concentration camp
the lecturer tells me
– she was a jewess
   must have been about 9 or 10 years old
   when they killed her
he adds

myself
i didnt like to see her poor hand floating there
whilest we ate our french breakfast
the yellowing tendon sawn thru
and
a tattooed number still showing on the
stub of her rist

i come with shin bones like knives

it is wonderful being a man
and
washing your body down at the sink
in the early morning
with a flannel rough as a badgers arse
the
lite coming in thru the window
hair slightly thining on top
and
then
stepping out into the street
and being loved by your son
and loving him rite back
and drinking tea
and owning
several pairs of trousers
a beat up car
and
an array of hats
to have a wife
and dinner
and sex
and sleep
just like a grown up
and
shitting in the morning too
sometimes shaving
growing a mustash
and feeling the inside of your teeth
with your own tongue
i come with shin bones like
knives
a clay pipe in my throat

and verses for you all
becouse
this
is my shit
and it smells good to me

woodcutter

i am a woman woodcutter
cutting down these woods at nite
proudly wearing
my dead husbands jack boots
and wielding his axe

he went to war
and left me to milk the cows
he sliced my hart
i was cut so i too cut
i cut trees
teligraph poles
even
a panzer tank would
be no match for my axe

i am a woman woodcutter
cutting down men
with chattering machine gun fire
you alone are to blame:
the men who make war
because we beg you to kill for us

i am the person you dont
recognise in the mirror after
half a bottle of vodka
but my face is your face

i keep my blade keen
and anoint it with fresh goose blud
i am the bad ending to every
fairy tail

the un ready

im not ready
for the woods of my childhood
to be obliterated
for these streets
to be smashed down
and
childrens hands to be raised
to the sky

im not ready for skool
and bullies
or my mother to tell me
over breakfast
that my fathers left home

im not ready
for teachers who dont love me
or decimelisation
or cctv cameras
endlessly watching

im not ready for you to hate me
or leave me
or for your love
or forgiveness
or for christ
or buddah
or prostitutes
or the clap and this nite

im not ready for un-payable morgages
pension plans
digital camaras

the death of the horse
the building of vast
shopping complexes
im not ready for the fake air
of airports
and you to ring me on a cell phone

im not ready for the skin of my hands to
fall like rice paper
or my jaw to crack
or to live in a wardrobe
or grow lumps in my neck and body
like grandfather lewis
or for my nana lewis to die
or for graying hair
falling hair
broken teeth
and woolworths of gillingham
to rip out their wooden floor boards

im not ready for the ice-caps to melt
or for punishment
or the sorrow of my mother
or her kisses
or to listen to the mannered voices of poets
killing me and killing lite

i feel myself younger than everybody
i meet

im not ready for this
i am not ready

a brimful of being

on a glorius track
upon a bridge spanning
the thames
i see life is an
arrangement of stones
seen from a passing train

a movement of matter
a lite display of
monsterous preportions
a flutter of strange wings
an infinitesimal delicacy
tiny meaningful
and
prefound

a brimful of being –
expansive
irrapressable –
not to be scorned
or blindly messured
but honoured
and loved rite back

the
person
sometimes
known
as
billy
childish

was in a hospital ward
acomponying a young lady
who was visiting her dying grandmother
whod raised the girl as her own

when the young lady saw the grandmother
she let out a sob
and ran crying from the ward
i went and fetched her
and comforting her
led her back to the bed telling her
that this wasnt about her
but about the old ladys death

i sat with the 2 of them
the old and the young
assuring the dying lady
(who i had not before met)
that she could do whatever she needed to do
and that he – the person sometimes known as billy
childish –
would look after the young lady
and all along i new i was lying but
it was a good lie
a true lie

devine conception

a red road spans a bridge at nite time
its steal arches high flung like
the wings of some great white bird

a lite flys there also
casting
its green blue lite
adding upon those god colours already
luminesent

this bridge is
an ancient causeway
softly trodden
by all who dare cross this blud gate
stepping with tender
knees
feeling fingers
and budding toes

listen!
another spirit is coming
curled there
beneath the great thrusting wings
feeling the blud warmth
on its cheek
waighting for gods call

the angry and the disallowing

disallowing blud
they come
disallowing mistakes
breath
and movement
disallowing
sensation
and
ants

disallowing ice
heat
leaves and greece and geece
disallowing nite and day
and the very seasons
disallowing mighty mamels and
lowly crawlers

disallowing the dislocated
the disstorted
and sperm

listen you fearful
know that every seed is counted
and breathed upon
like ancient coins by the breath
of gods

and so you will be
disallowed

its god again
the fucker

god is a devil
godding me
god is a devil
living me
its god again
the old fucker

its butifull to have a body
to shit
and
piss
and
cum

to walk
and
dream of endless orgasam
to eat till you puke of it
and drink
and fart
and stagger
and
laugh too hard
and
unrealisticly

to cook up poems for jackels
and fools
and
love god sat there a be-feathered bird
singing in a burning bush
and
then to spring on my magical hands
and toes
and
have my teeth drilled
and
know that sometime soon
in the impossible futcher it will all end
only to begin again
to be gods butifull body

to have him live you
and
wonder

sabalius and gods goose

deep down in his finish hart
he knew that gods goose
thought he was a lousy violinist

he stomped his fat fingers on the keys of his piano
and
watched them bouncing off like raw potatoes
he sat back
lit a cigar
got blind drunk
slept with a prostitute
and had his throat slit open
all this
just to imitate
the honking voice
of that damned goose

– whats got into you
asked his astonished pals
– whats rong with quacking like a duck
   or arnt ducks good enough for you?

– no it must be a grey goose! he spat

and
with that he tossed his prized violin into the firey flames
and
rocked there crying like a big girl as it fizzed into ashe

next morning his wife watched as he
carreened around the garden
– if i cant sing like a goose
   then i am at least going to dress like al capone

he sulked
the idiot had even shaved his bulit-like head

and
out arcross the brooding fjords
came the bark bark bark of the grey goose

gods hand

black as charcole dust
dipping ochre
and
bison fat
it
pattens the walls of
ice bound caves
in a 100,000 year winter
then
deftly draws
a summer birch tree
a summer dove
blud
sap
and
time
condensed
in gods hand

EMOTIONAL SECRETIONS

hear i stand

hear i stand
22
one mother – sweet
one father – fucked
one brother – successful
with an education
as clean and as long
as his arm

hear i stand
22
worts on my cock
(the doctor burned the
ones off my arse)
100 paintings
a couple of hundred
poems
2 dead teeth
gonnareah and hurpis
i think ive got
excilent qualifactions

poetry and wood

there will be a time when you
are not here to read this
there will be a time when this
earth is blasted back into the
rock from which it was formed

there will be a time –
years and years of countless
seconds –
this world has lived without
us before and it will live
without us again
this is as sure and as
important as the death of a
slug

there will be a time – i know
when there wont be these women
ive acumilated queueing to be
fucked
there will be dry years
long dry years and a death
that i can only guess at

there will be a time when im
not driveing thru the nite
on a push bike with no lites
no air in the tiers
drunk on snake bite guinnes
wisky and rum with a carrier bag
full of wood blocks depicting a
life

woodblocks and this poem

outside my window is the poor
frozen city
cars wont start – chaos!
water pipes burst – catastrophy!
the poor humans are in turmoil

i piss in the frozen toilet downstairs
then leave my home
i walk away from my work
(woodblocks and this poem)

i spend 3 days or more away
i get drunk on my social security
check
after the wisky maybe ile walk
myself back here in the dead of
nite without my knowing

next morning hungover
and the
toilet downstairs still held
in its block of ice
but the werk is done
something is fixed in words or
wood

this is my method
im not talking about jigsaw
puzzels or lituary traditions
im talking about sneeking up on
your own soul

dead funny

i am a thorn in the side
of the establishment

my success annoys everyone
to the extent that even i pretend
not to be successful

my adolescent concerns
are the bore of the town
my friends hiss at me
and ex-lovers wish me dead

honestly even my own mother
cant bear to read my texts

it seems ive painted a lot of shit
so much so that i meet complete strangers
who presume that i swim in it with glee

and with every poem i rite
my fame grows
another nail in my coffin
people feel embarrassed for me
everything i utter becomes a cliché

when oh when the people ask
will billy shut up

the billy childish

i am billy childish
ex drunk
and compulsive masturbator
late nite vomiter of good liquor
kisser of purple lipped women
riter of poems celebrating the
emptiness of my love
poems hungering for the moment
of my passion
wishing it could allways be so
to never let my cock fall

i am billy childish
ex strongman
and 2-bit lover
late nite namer of names
corrupter of the literate
riter of poems that dare
to dream to pass down
the centurys
and touch the harts of the
the yet-to-be-born
wishing to hold them
to my arms
and kiss them all

i am billy childish
ex-poet
and failed suiside
late nite vomiter of truth and lies
kisser of the arses of girls
like the stars of god
riter of poems to lick

the thighs of the dead
for ex-lovers to denounce
and teachers to hate
wishing to paint my life
and to never let my
voice quieten

the shed

my car is a 68 volvo estate
given me by my brother
painted seaweed green
drinks a gallon of oil a week
he hands over the keys
– theres a special way of opening the bonnit
he tells me
– and the back door doesnt lock
   and the rear window
   doesnt wind up
   youll have to jam it with something
   heres a spair key
   if you can find anyone who still cuts them
   get more cut
   becouse they snap off in the ignition
   i keep a spair in the ashe tray
   in case of imergences
   get some gaffer tape
   becouse the back number plates almost off
   and youll need a plastic bag over your leg
   becouse the rain leeks in round the wind shield
   and it dips over the exsalerator
   and when you put in the petrol
   only fill it a quarter full
   otherwise the tank leeks

– other than that
   it goes pritty good
   oh yes
   and its called the shed

*ps the drivers side rear lite is smashed out and
taped over with a red malteaser packet*

the wounded poet

who is meaner
funnier
and
more perverse than me
who is so childlike
so far seeing
and
narrower
than myself
who is so desscreet
so indecent
and such a blabber mouth

who is more cruel
and
loving
who could be as hard
and sentimental
who is so much in need
of uplifting and praise
whos ego so rampant
yet self seen

what poet can better me
in battle
and where is there a finer
more compleat artist
than myself

who
in the history of the world
has ever seen themselfs so low
in their own estermations

or been so bostful
impudent
and shy

who has been so cut from god
yet joined with god
who has asked so many fine questions
and supplied such sparkling answers

who has embraced so many women
and fellows
and helped so many lost poets

who has made such a
sumptious banquet of himself
beqithed his bones
to the yet-to-be-born
made such a feast of his flesh for the angry
the impoverished of soul
and haters
of simple art

i am the un corrected

becouse
i cant spell
and
refuse to show off
with cheep tricks
and
still allow myself to paint
like a monky
i
am not elevated

fear me

becouse
i have no certificates
refused to be educated
and
my riting style is free
true
and easy
yet
i have ritten novels
that disgust the sences
i
am not elevated

fear me

i
am gloryiously
un corrected
and will
be coming for you
next

knight of the sad face

in this town
where
i
have lost
several teeth
a note book containing poetry
of a personal nature
the paintings of my youth
3 girlfriends
a
pocketful
of
lose change
my fathers
yellow hair
my claim to genius
a small screw
a pair of stollen sissors
reasons
belief
and
the buttons off my overcoat

i have found
a piece of cheap jewelry
on a hillside
belonging to a crying
indian girl
afraid of being beaten by her mother

hearing her sobs
i stand and walk 20 paces
look down

and there it is at my feet
i
pick up the bracelet
call to her
and
drop it glinting into her smiling palm
she turns and runs laughing to her friends
all dressed in shimmering saris

they leave the field
and
i am left looking after them
this knight of the sad face

i am a knight of honour

yes
i set lite to your hair
and
yes
i punched you in the jaw
and
yes
i got married behind your back
and
yes
i rote those awful poems about us
of our nites of passion
and how mean spirited you were
and
yes
i destroyed the only 3 love letters
that i ever sent you
(i broke into your flat
whilest you pretended
to be living on a barge
in amsterdam
and
burnt them in the fire place)
and
yes
i refused to marry you
and settle down and have children
with you
and
yes
i picked you up by the stomach
and thru you across
the floor

and
you lost a child
that you never told me you were
carrying
and yes i gave you a dose of
gohnareah
when i slept with that
german prostitute
and yes i refused to have sex with you
and
yes
i slept with that japanese girl
begging her to save me from the
otterman empire
and
when you asked me to lie
i did my best to lie
and
yes
i spoke with that
idiotic newspaper
when you swore at me not to
which was rong of me
but
sweet hart
i never
punched you as hard as i let you
punch me
and
there
are so many other ways
in which i was hurt
as well
but i speak of this
and
admit to this

not for your tears
but
becouse
i am a knight of honour
and you
are not

billy childish cant paint

there will be
an exhibition of new paintings
by billy childish
followed by a master class
in creativity by britons
werst artist

applicants must hate art
despise poetry
but have an otherwise cheery disposition

no music permited

advert in the times

tall charismatic young man (47)
seeks fame and fortune in the arts/is willing to curb
his rudness and say sorry
interests
yoga
meditation
and war

i live the perfict life of a poet

no wonder
everyones jellouse of me
i live the perfict life
of a poet

traveling the world
hating airports
cars
and telivision sets

dismissing great authors
with never having read them
ridiculing
pop musians
and
artists
that i couldnt be bothered to listen to
or look at

showing off in my poets hat
riting with my special authors pen
growing a mustash
and marrying a red indian

and
theres allways plenty
to write off
my drunken father
mice in the kitchen
my bullying big brother
and
i am dislexic too
uneducated

expelled from art skool
alcoholic
sexaholic
riting on the train
drawing on the train
my poems
smiling on
unknown strangers
who mock me
and
so
i live this perfict life
of
a poet
uncontained

for 15 years
i was painting and riting on the dole
and my mother allways said
– billy doesnt really do anything
and when she read my poetry
she said
– you must lern not to antogonise people
and
thou i was 21 i would still steal coins from her purse
like i was a 12 year old
most people i think
would agree with her

the reason is of course
is that i am uncontained

the
forever
moving
target

– dont trust the poets
said nietzcher
– they lie too much

theres the truth
give the barstards short shrift
bugger their special world view
shit on their overblown dramas
piss on their drugs experences
their whoring
conquests
defeats
thugery
and special vision

of
course theyle be upsets
and tears
theres allways upsets and tears
and
acusations
reprisels
and blame apportioned

but thats what its like
dealing with liers
and poets

**emotional truth is the lie of all art
and
all poetry**

dont give me your bull
about emotional truth
go fuck your emotional truth
this
is truthful emotion

townsman of a different age

on
your evening stroll
did you ever dream
the
futcher towns
could hold this:
trashed and drug strewn
churches closed up
pubs gone
the empire theater raised

your
enimys
teaming
the nite streets of rotted teeth
your
grand age ground to a close
your extravigent
decorations
and
qualitys
deemed
waistful
retarded and retrograde
your
tradition amounting to naught
but
this sweet fragrence
was already on the nite air
the flower budded
in all that you valued
all you needed to do was sniff

a plague of
hot blud

i suffered gum boils that burst
and
filled my mouth with blud
and
boils on my legs
and
back
i was bandaged
and hobbeled
just a little boy
2 or 3 years old
and
my mother holding me down
as
my father burst the puss
out of me

cave art

as a child
i was against eating
later
i loathed skool
and
english

unable to spell
and
refusing food i
vomited
naturally art was
my
favorite

looking to cave paintings
wooly rhinos
mamoth
and the ochre
handprints
of
those too smart to read

i never use a pencil sharpener

i have had many lifes
in this strange life
many idears
and
strange behaviours
strange abuse
strange neglect
strange love
stray dogs
gonnareah
herpis
alcholisim
and
ritten
revenge

naturally
i have wonky teeth
and
never once owned a micro-wave
and
when
sat drawing
on our sleek modern trains
(where like children we are no longer trusted
to open doors or windows)
my weapon of choice is allways my trusted pen
knife
in
this respect
i also
use my own spit to lubricate my cock and water
colours

and
have allways shined my brillience from within
like gods radient flower
pissing off
miners
scafolders
artists
and
poets
and
where the winners
worship art
i stand at the back and see nothing
it
must be
that their brains
are like the finest sieved white flour

im not sure my mind werks
like a poem
or that i even want it to
where so many people want to identify themselves
as artist
poet
mucisan
i want to jump ship
i mean
ive never even learned my A B C
at 56 i still get lost somewhere around 'Q'
and
my slim hold
on reading and riting
is all i got at 14
(about the same time i stopped pissing the bed)
you see
i was messed with

i was ment to become a good victim
or
surviver
or
a poet
but i refused
cant you tell
youve
got the rong man
im happier
just pushing the brush

waiting
to become

talent is
common place
luck
(or gods grace)
underated

everywhere
people are queuing to become
someone

deriding god
they
dont even know
that
god is what
they are seeking

poets
artists
musicians

all
craving to win
to
feel others eyes
crawl over them
and
so be uplifted
and
completed
in others envy

unholdeble

it seams
that maybe i should rite a poem
about loss
about suicides that have come to close
(all men
all recent)

yes
it seams
that maybe i should rite a poem
about the gaping hole
i still feel in life (in myself)
and
how i am reminded
that no matter
how much
i want to hold the world safe next to me
(even thru this poem)
the days open
and explode of their own will
unholdeble

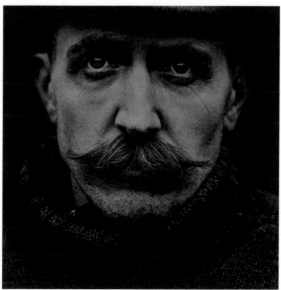

Billy Childish was born in Chatham, Kent in 1959. After leaving secondary school at sixteen, he worked at Chatham Dockyard as an apprentice stonemason. Initially denied an interview for the local art school, during six months of employment at the dockyard he produced hundreds of drawings that gained him entry to St Martin's School of Art. Mr Childish's defiance to authority and his insistence on integrity and personal style above the formalities of educational requirement led to his eventual expulsion from art school in 1981.

Mr Childish then embarked on an artistic, literary and musical odyssey exploring a broad range of worldly themes including war, history, social protest and religious philosophy, as well as his own experience of alcoholism and the sexual abuse he suffered as a child. With over forty years of continual creative activity, Mr Childish has gained a cult status worldwide; he has written and published five novels and over seventy volumes of confessional poetry, recorded over 150 albums, and has received international critical acclaim for his work as a painter.

June 2018

This first edition is published as a
trade paperback; there are 50 numbered
copies signed by the poet & handbound in
boards by the Tangerine Press, Tooting, London;
numbered copies also contain an original
two colour woodcut by Billy Childish.